Released, Redeemed, Renewed:
Discover How to Live In Freedom Every Day

— Newly Revised Edition —

Live by
Design
Not by Default

R^3 L.I.F.E

Live by *Design!* Not by Default

REDEEMED

RELEASED

RENEWED

Discover how to
Live In Freedom Every Day

Presented by
Drs. Anthony & Kim Ladson

Dratladson@gmail.com or Kimladson@aol.com

Ordering Information

Individual Sales: www.livebydesignthebook.com

Quantity Sales: Special discounts are available in quantity purchases by corporations, associations, and networking groups. For details contact us at the address above or call:

1-845 288-3068 or 212-498-9271
www.livebydesignthebook.com

Book cover by ButterflyGrapix
Revised edit and book interior by Jean Boles
https://www.upwork.com/fl/jeanboles

Table of Contents

Acknowledgement

This book was written to reach those who are harnessed and need to be **Released,** those who are in debt to life and desire to be **Redeemed** and those that are looking to be **Renewed** in order to

Live In Freedom Every Day.

Live by

Design

Not by Default

An Introduction To LIFE

Live by
Design!
Not by Default

By Drs. Kim and Anthony Ladson

"One of the greatest discoveries a man makes, one of his great surprises, is to find he can do what he was afraid he couldn't do."

— Henry Ford

An Introduction To Life
By Drs. Kim and Anthony Ladson

What does life really mean? Life is living, breathing, walking and operating in what we were created to do. Life is living your WHY. Mark Twain said that the two most important dates in our lives are the day we were born and the day we discover our WHY. This book is about discovering that WHY, pursuing that WHY, and sharing that WHY with the world. Along the way, we will experience bumps, bruises, obstacles, hurdles and many inconveniences, but our core desire, as we exist in separate and different cultures, is to discover that Why and to live it without question or apology.

Living our WHY is all about loving and being loved, about operating within significance. The purpose of life and the reality of life is to be happy, to be at peace, to experience joy fully and unapologetically. Freedom is that sense of living.

When we are born and reach that first year where our understanding becomes clear, we begin to see choices presented to us. Those choices may become the bondage that we must escape from at some point in life—bondage of other people's opinions, other people's feelings, other people's goals, aspirations and dreams.

You see, we often begin living for others, living the dreams and the designs of other people. Our perception does not get a chance to be a part of the equation until we come to that point of understanding. Freedom is that sense of living, that sense of understanding, that sense of knowing.

As a child, we ate what was presented to us without question. Adults cooked us collard greens and cakes; they presented both to us, and we were told to like them. It is only when we get further along in life that we get to make the decision if we indeed like both or either.

I'm reminded of the story of the mother and daughter that were cooking a ham together. The daughter asked her mom, **"Why do we always cut the end of the ham off before we put it in the pan?"** The mother said, **"Well I don't know, baby; that's what my mother always did, let's**

ask her." So they called the grandmother and she said, **"Well, my mother always did. The reason she cut the ends off the ham was so that it would fit into the only pan that she had."** All this time I thought the ham tasted good and was delicious because the ends were cut off. Although that was the perception, it was not the truth. In life, we were given many traditions and customs and were told that they were right.

In life, we are given many traditions, customs and mores and told that they are reality. After all, everyone else does it, or did it, so you might as well too. There's no concept of why life becomes about fitting in the pan. At some point, we will come to the understanding that cutting did not make the ham taste better, that was just the choice made to make it fit. You should make a choice, are you fitting into someone else's pan or are you living someone else's life? Have you decided to begin to live your own life? To follow your own purpose? To define your dream?

What you see will be limited to the perceptions that you've received from others and those whom you surround yourself with. It's possible to design a life to fit in bigger pans. We really are designed for larger pans. Live life so that it fits your dream. Live life so that it doesn't have to be cut down to fit another's dream, but it can be given a chance to grow and be all it wants to be. You see, freedom doesn't fit into a confined mold. Freedom is something that is unique, and it allows the individual to see life in a different way.

Freedom causes you to see another side of the struggle, another side of the pain, another side of the tears. **The other side is freedom, is joy, is the ultimate life. The ultimate life is not in the pursuit or the fullness of the material things. It is about the vision, the goal, and the dream being realized. Why not wake up to freedom?** Don't cut or shave off your vision to get another one, to get another why or look for another way? You can have what you want if you know what you want.

There is a **Guideline to Greatness**. I guarantee you that greatness will not happen overnight. It will not happen in a day, but it will happen daily. It is the things you do every day, the small steps you take that will lead you to your greatness. It is in the small moments you take daily to read, to pray, to write, to work on yourself, and to connect with others that build you up. The more you say yes to your dreams, the more your dreams will say yes to you. If it is done daily, it becomes the lifestyle, the lifestyle becomes the freedom that you're seeking, and that you know exists.

That allows us to Live In Freedom Every Day. There are three elements to that life...to be **Released, Redeemed and Renewed**. To live life released means that you design your life so that it is not lived by default. It means being released from the old way of thinking. For as you know, the Bible states, **As a Man Thinketh in his heart so he is**. Thinking creates bondage when you think lack, scarcity, or defeat. You will begin to live in lack, scarcity and defeat.

When you surround yourself with those who think better, who have abundant thinking, then you will have abundant results. When you surround yourself with people that have more, that want more, that desire more and are developing more than you are, you can look forward to being released from the *stinking thinking* that was holding you back. The thinking that told you that all you have is all you will ever have and that is enough for you. Release your mind from hatred, from lack, from depression, from frustration and instead fill it with joy, with peace, with possibilities of success, and you'll start seeing that as the reality of your life.

This leads us to Redemption. Christ paid it all, but you should let go and release and allow the redemption to occur. Redemption is a gained result—you gain self-esteem, you gain service to yourself and to others. Webster defines redemption as to recover ownership by paying the price required. There is a price all of us must pay to be released from the past. We must be redeemed in order to recover ownership of our self and to be able to go to the place that we desire to be.

We can gain ownership of who we are, we can recover our purpose if we let go, and we'll find restoration to the ultimate essence of man, which is greatness. Redemption restores us to our position of power, prominence, and purpose.

This leads us to Renew. When I think about the concept of renewal, I ask the question: "It's got to be more _____ than this." More to life, more to church, more to love, more to living, there must be more to it than this. Renewal of thinking that produced the old fruit is what is required to be able to have that new life. Renewed thought equals a renewed result. This leads to new fruit from your new way of thinking. Thoughts create results, which create better fruit. You must plant, then you should water, and when it becomes ripe, you have to reap the results that you are looking for.

Renewal brings a change to your whole life. It creates the love you have been lacking and gives you evidence of all you have been expecting. The old thoughts say that if you want a house, go get a mortgage and pay it off in 30 years. The term mortgage means pay off until you die. A renewed mind would change that and you begin to see a better result. It's about realizing that everything is controlled by the mind. Everything around us can be renewed.

We can move from **I can't, to I can,** we can repurpose and begin picking up the purpose that we laid down. Begin again to have courage to write that book, to take that class, to take that seminar, to go to that conference and to meet new people. What you said you couldn't do, now you can do, because now with a renewed mind you have the action to accomplish your ambition. You must be **okay with being uncomfortable** and then you become comfortable with the **new renewed** you.

We want to thank you for reading this book. We want to say that this is the book, if you allow it to, that can change your life and your way of thinking. **It will release you, redeem you and renew you to a completely new life**. Then you can begin living in freedom every day.

Preface

Read this book one chapter at a time. Each author was carefully chosen to share with you and present to you a slice of his or her soul. Each story is a separate expression of what it means to undertake and overtake the excesses of life. You **CAN** Live in Freedom Every Day. The answer is that you must know what you desire and realize that you can have the desire of your heart. This is not just a spiritual book (although it is), it is not just a Self-Help book (although it is), this is a book that gives everyone an option for winning based on beginning the process needed to win. We challenge you to **Live In Freedom Every Day**. All you have to do is **Release, Redeem and Renew.**

From Special To Great

Live by
Design!
Not by Default

By Dr. Anthony Ladson

"Get action. Do things. Be sane, don't fritter away your time. Create. Act. Take a place wherever you are and be somebody."

— Theodore Roosevelt

From Special
To Great

By Dr. Anthony Ladson

There was a popular song several years ago entitled *OPP*. Many of the connotations of that song are not appropriate for positive conversation. Yet, I see it from another distinction. To me it means *Other People's Perspectives.*

You see, people have opinions and viewpoints about you that don't necessarily reflect you. Other People's Perspectives shape your life and shake your image. As we grow up from childhood to adulthood, Other People's Perspectives play a lot into who we become and what we accept as our reality.

In many cases, things we do and the actions we take are shaped by the perspectives that others have given us regarding what they feel our life should be, could be and would be. In most cases, we did not do what we wanted to do, but what we felt we should do to please those that had perspectives and viewpoints on us that they felt were important.

Our parents, our teachers, even our friends held perspectives that became reflective of who we were and who we were to become. To be truly free, you must be led by your own perspective, your own image of yourself. Moreover, while there is nothing wrong with getting advice from other people, ultimately, we have to decide what to do with that advice and whether or not we want to move forward on it.

In dealing with Other People's Perspectives, it often becomes necessary to react rather than respond to their expectations of you—how you should live with it, how you should deal with reality. Over time, I began to see that pastors and churches give their perspective of how you should act. They will give you their perspective on the Bible and on life itself. In addition, although many cases involve them being called, and/or studying seriously to get an understanding of God's Word, it ultimately was their perspective on that Word that shaped their opinions.

The same religious leaders feel it's okay to approve or disapprove actions taken by their congregants. This leads to bondage and lack of freedom. You get pigeonholed into a certain perspective that they gave you—in other words, their opinion. This often ends up with people programming their life according to the viewpoints, opinions and expectations of others.

I have coached many of my clients that they should live the life they design, not the life of default that many find themselves succumbing to. In living life by default, we acquiesce to what our friends, parents, teachers, pastors and others dictate as being correct. So rather than being creative, in essence, we became reactive. That reactive mindset causes us to not engage in designing a life at all, but rather living a life designed by others. You should become the real designer of your own life. In addition, oftentimes that design can take place after reacting to the expectations, viewpoints and perspectives of others.

When you live life by default, you are living according to Other People's Perspectives. When you live life by design, you are receiving what you feel your life should, could and must be. You see, every second operates off of *now*. Now is the time you get to design your future. The only time that you can effectively design or create the world that you want to live in is a time called now.

You might ask how this is done. It is done by not considering Other People's Perspectives. By not responding to, or receiving what other people have **dictated and designed for you.**

You should begin with a blank slate every day. Even now we're writing and filling on that slate to create and design the life that we want, **that we deserve and that we decide upon.**

When my father died in my arms and I was unable to help him, that was a traumatic experience for me. Thus, I became defiant and tried to fight everyone around me, including my family, friends, teachers and even the principal. This created a negative perspective with Other People's Perspectives about my life. I spiraled so far out of control that the administrators and teachers thought I had lost my mind. After talking with my mother and me, it was decided that I should attend special education classes. They presented this alternative to me and stated that I would have special attention in smaller classes. I would get access to a greater level of work since my grades were not a problem. This appealed to me enough so much that I looked forward to attending those classes.

On the first day of classes, as I walked down a narrow, dimly lit hall, away from the normal classes that the other students and my friends were attending, I knew something was wrong. My emotional life was out of control. Yet more importantly, I began to see my new educational component as having a stigma attached to it. It **looked bleak and uncomfortable.**

As I headed to this new place of confinement, I became confused and conflicted. I tried to back out even from the very first day, feigning a necessity to go to the restroom, and/or back to the school bus to get my lunch. They told me that there was a restroom in the classroom and that lunch was provided for me. As I peered into the room through the class window, I was shocked at the sight I saw. I saw this kid with a funny shaped head and crossed eyes looking back at me with a blank stare as if he was saying, "Welcome home my friend."

For years, I experienced the stigma of special education, and every waking day I wanted to break out of the shackles that it provided me. That perspective that other people had of me based on my special education classification was that I was crazy, slow, and placed in *special education* for my own good and for the good of the rest of the students.

As I began to live out that slow-class concept, my behavior expressed it. I developed low self-esteem. I wanted out; I didn't belong to be categorized that way, yet people labeled me as such—the dumb guy. My mindset soon became that *I was the dumb guy*. I began to change, and it shaped the image that I had of myself.

Even though my paradigm was being changed and molded into something that I didn't want, I knew this one thing for sure: I did not belong in that program and I didn't see myself as slow. I began to look for a way out. As I looked back on that time, I remembered my good friend and mentor Les Brown was in a similar situation. Moreover, just like him I did not perform to the image of myself. I wanted out and was finally able to get out.

I would not accept the image they were putting on me. They saw things from their perspective and felt that I was crazy, stupid, slow etc. However, I knew that I was brilliant, incredible, and destined for greatness. My friends would laugh and taunt that they would not put me in that class unless I deserved to be there and that I was crazy and slow.

I was staged there in that place where they thought someone like me belonged. As they began to speak these negative, low self-esteem images of me, I began to fight back. You see, life and death is indeed in the tongue. Greatness lives or dies based on how the people perceive and predict you to be. When authority figures say that you are slow, you begin to believe it. The tongues of all those around me rolled up to condemn me. Yet I didn't receive that condemnation, and I began to see myself as successful, see myself as getting out of that stigmatized place.

Default is what others see and say about you, and you accept it. Living the default life is doing, being, and becoming what others say you are. Living the default life is accepting Other People's Perspectives of what **they say you can or cannot do.**

People have pre-conceived opinions and perspectives about you and everything around you. I remember going to purchase a car for my wife and telling the salesperson that I planned to pay cash for it. His perspective was that doing so was a dumb move. "Nobody pays cash; you should just put a decent down payment and make payments over time. You can save and invest that money and earn a great interest for yourself. Why should you pay all that money up front?"

I looked at it from a different perspective. I realized that by paying cash I no longer had a monthly payment. More importantly, I saw it as a way for freedom to not have to be worried every month about making that payment, even if I could. I decided what was smart for them may not be smart for me. In many cases, making that monthly payment was a way for the salesperson and the dealership to get additional finance money off my monthly payment. That was his opinion that it was better for me, but I realized in many cases it was better for them.

In most cases, other people's opinions are designed for you to benefit them and not yourself. To accept another person's perspective of you, without deciding whether it is beneficial to you, could be detrimental to you. What's good for them may not be best for you.

You see, at some point there must be a paradigm shift. You must begin looking at things from a perspective of what's in it for you. People benefit when you act on their perspective rather than your own. Authority figures tell you what's best for you when in essence it is best for them. Do your research and review to see who benefits the most from the actions of the perspective they want you to engage in. Who gets blessed, them or you? The eyes they see you as—perceive you to be—is what they want to design your life to be. They want you to run, to jump and to behave when you are advised to do it because it benefits them in the end.

Again, I say it is important that you seek the advice of others. Nevertheless, Other People's Perspectives don't have to become the elective that you choose. The Bible says a wise man seeks the counsel of many and a fool seeks the advice of none. Once you've sought the advice of others, it is up to you to decide what to do with it.

People will share with you a negative perspective of your own life based on how they see you, not how you see yourself. No one can ever know the real you, that *you on the inside*. Einstein, when he was in school, was labeled as slow and was considered dumb. Col. Sanders was considered too old to start a business, and Henry Ford was told that it was impossible to create the V-8 engine. Other People's Perspective of you may be that you're too dumb, too slow—too this, too that.

The key to freedom is to believe in your own perspective. To shape, design and create your own perspective of yourself. Walt Disney was fired and told he had no imagination, yet if he had received and accepted that perspective we would never have had Disney World or all the wonderful characters he created. In retrospect, he is now a genius. He's a genius because he stepped forward, and all the others—Henry Ford and the like—stepped forward and would not accept Other People's Perspectives of themselves.

The turning point in gaining freedom is that you must take introspection rather than the perspective of others. You must look within yourself and become sick and tired of suppressing your freedom and your gift. How often have you been told that you're not good enough and that now is not the right time?

The turning point begins when you decide to design your own life from your own perspective.

The inner knowing, that inner voice that says if others are doing it I can do it also. Outside opinions versus the inside perspective must begin with the understanding that you have greatness within yourself. You must begin on the journey to believing in yourself. To knowing that you have something special that you can share with the world.

You may not be able to fully explain it to the world but you know inside that there is something great. You must see yourself as special; you must have an image of yourself doing what you know you can do.

Words create pictures, and what people say about you when they express an opinion creates a picture in your mind. You see yourself as what they said you are. Every word paints a new picture of who you are. Those words paint a picture in your mind. They may say that you are fat when you are as thin as you can be. Soon, you begin to see that image of yourself as being fat, and that becomes the reality. That image in your mind transforms you into what you have seen yourself to be.

When you can see the image of yourself—that picture in your mind—as other than that which you have been categorized, you begin a transformation at that point. You must say, *"I am what I say I am, not what you say I am."* You must create and develop a positive perspective of your own life. You must see yourself as special in your own mind and hold onto that image.

Many people have an image that they did not design. I always have said that *we live by design or by default.* We live by negative or positive faith. We often don't hear about negative faith, only positive faith. Nevertheless, when people speak negative things about us to us, it creates a negative faith about that thing. You must have the faith that you can do all things. It is also a negative faith that says you can't, and whether it is negative or positive, that faith creates that reality.

In many cases, someone else may have a better perspective or image of you than you have of yourself. That's a positive perspective. You see the perspective that you accept because of what you want to be, what you operate by, what you believe in.

Don't receive the negative report. Someone else's blueprint, order or command will then become a reality in your life. Their advice can lead to failure, but it also can lead to your success.

When you have cheerleaders in your life, such as your family, your wife or even your kids, you can have a positive **OPP**. That cheerleader or friend that has a positive perspective can help you to keep pushing forward so you can reach your hopes and dreams. Just as that negative *fear leader* can prevent you from being who you were designed to be.

Who you allow in your triangle of trust determines your life. Those that you surround yourself with or allow to be close to you are speaking words in your life. Be careful that those words are positive and that they speak positive possibilities into your life. Make sure that they are aligned with the image that you hold of yourself and that you want to see manifest in your life. They should have no access to your future, into your life, if they don't hold your best interest at heart.

I leveraged my negative self-image and reality to a positive one. I did this by massive suggestions to myself. I was able to design the life that I desired. I look at **Other People's Perspectives,** but I choose my own. The power to define is the power to fulfill. I ask myself, is this a success or failure image representation of me?

You must constantly consider everything that people say to you. There are six ways that **OPP** damages your life.

   1. Their expectation causes us to be obligated to live up to them or to their expectations.

   2. No one knows you better than yourself

   3. Only you can define what's possible for you.

   4. Freedom is living life your own way, not by other people's standards

   5. Not living in that freedom is damaging to your life and your goals and your dreams.

   6. You are obligated to others more than yourself when you begin living according to their expectations and perspectives.

We offer our unconscious mind/self and allow that unconsciousness to dictate our life without a conscious consideration of creativity. *The design life is the divine life.* So how do you gain freedom in life and begin living in freedom every day?

There are four basic standards of Freedom Living

1. Realize that you are good enough.

Know that you are good enough to operate on your own and achieve and receive the dreams and goals of life. It is important that you tell yourself that you're good enough, that you're not worthless, that you are worthy of the dreams and goals that you set for yourself.

2. Your perspective matters.

All around you people are giving you their opinions, their expectations, their perspectives of you and your life. The important thing to consider is that your perspective matters, your perspective is important. You see, we are already tested in the furnace of life and what remains after the burning away is the core value of our own importance.

3. Embrace your creativity.

To gain freedom in life you have to realize that the worst thing you can do is to betray yourself and deny your dreams. Create the life worth living by designing your dreams from within.

4. Let go and be B.O.L.D.

Be bold enough to walk away from negative images that others are trying to place on you. To accept yourself as you see yourself.

Believe in that image,

Own that image,

Love yourself,

Decide that this is the image of who you are.

We must ask the most important question, which is... **Why Am I**!

We can look at our life and say I am this or I am that, but the question that must be asked is, **Why Am I**? Why am I bold, why am I successful, why am I living in freedom every day? Once you answer the **why**, everything else comes into perspective.

Bio:

Dr. Anthony T. Ladson is a John Maxwell Certified leadership Speaker/Trainer and Coach who helps executives, marketplace leaders, and senior pastors reduce the stress and frustration associated with the gap that exists between their faith in God and their corporate actions and responsibilities.

Utilizing the PLATINUM LEADERSHIP OF EXCELLENCE Formula, a proprietary methodology designed specifically to address how Christian leaders can be high performance leaders who are capable of building and sustaining high performance teams while maintaining their ethical and moral standards, Dr. Anthony T. Ladson can improve leadership performance by providing solutions that are elegantly simple, yet highly effective.

Contact Info:

Dratladson@gmail.com
1-846-288-3068

My Story

Live by *Design*! Not by Default

By Desiree Wicker

"Bloom where you're planted."

— Mary Engelbreit

My Story
By Desiree Wicker

Being at a place of satisfaction in who you are, or who you are becoming, I believe happens or evolves in stages. At least that's what happened to me.

I can honestly say that my *becoming* came late in life. I never felt like I was missing anything, but I was. I let life happen to me and I did nothing to participate; I would just go with the flow. Whatever life threw at me I caught and dealt with it. Don't get me wrong, I was in Christ and believed His Word and knew I could live a life of victory. But I had no idea that there was so much more. I had life, but what I was missing was ABUNDANCE.

I believe it was in my late thirties that I began seeking for more. My prayer changed...I was looking for God to appear in my life based on the Word that I read and adored so much. I questioned how my life could look so different from what God was saying in His Word. Something was wrong, and I went on a journey for answers.

At this stage in my life I can say that I'm satisfied with who I'm becoming. The answer now is "YES." I don't live life haphazardly, but with everything, I seek out His purpose for my life. I no longer accept what is dealt to me without question. Abundance for me is living and pursuing my purpose, chasing after what God has placed on the inside of me. Everything that I do and say must match up and point me in the direction of my purpose.

I'm where I am today because of my search for answers. It was in the years of searching that God told me I would leave New York. He did not tell me where I would go until August of 2005. It was at this place called UNFAMILIAR where I truly learned to trust God and seek out my purpose. It was at this place that He let me know that I had value. It was at this place that I accepted His unconditional love. It was at this place that He matured me!

I thought the stage of UNFAMILIAR had started when I relocated to Georgia, but in fact it started the moment I began to search for more!

I was unprepared when I was dismissed from a church that I served in for ten years; this situation hit me and hurt me to my core and left a hole in my soul. Let me see if I can paint a clearer picture of why I was devastated. I'm the type of person that's all in—no half stepping. Every part of my being is invested, my time, energy, prayer, sacrifice, everything. If you tell me this is where we're going, then this is where we're going. I don't care what we face or how long it takes, because we're on our way to fulfill God's purpose.

This is how God worked it out. I stayed home one Sunday, which is not the norm for me. I cried as I looked in the mirror asking God, *"What do I do now?"* I told God that if I stayed out one more Sunday, it would be easy for me to walk away from church.

As I was still sitting at the edge of my bed, looking in the mirror, a statement that I had once made came back to me. "If I was not a member at another church, I would be right here." I had made this statement because I was in the office serving the First Lady, because of an outside engagement. The pastor was telling us all about this leadership class that was coming up, and that's when I made the statement.

Yes, God I remember the statement, but I don't remember the man nor the church. A few minutes later, I could see the man's face, but I still did not remember his name or the name of the church. A few minutes after that I remembered the church's name. The next day I called to find out their times of service and that is where I stayed for two years. I didn't know at the time, but that was the place God sent me to receive my healing and to continue my journey of the unfamiliar.

The next Sunday I attended church and sat in the back. I did not want anyone to ask me any questions. I wanted to go to service and leave, and that's exactly what I did for several Sundays. Once benediction was given, I was out the door. On this particular Sunday, the pastor was ending the service, but he was walking to the back of the church. In my mind, I'm thinking, *where is he going?* When he ends the prayer, he is standing right next to me; I could not escape. He looked at me as he shook my hand with a puzzled look on his face and said, "I know you." As I shook his hand I reminded him who—the church—I used to be connected with and quickly made my exit.

What I love about God is that He continues to work in our lives whether we're aware of it or not. The stage of UNFAMILIAR continued...a few months go by and I continue to attend and feel comfortable. There were two services and lunch was served in between. I would attend both services as well as eat in between. This Sunday I went upstairs, and I noticed that the Bishop's office was open. As I was in the line, the Bishop saw me. He called me into the office and introduced me to another member. The Bishop told the member, "She will be able to do that." Obviously, I came at the end of the conversation. The *she* was me and *that* was serving him. I left the office a little confused thinking "Where did that come from?"

I had no intention of serving in this church, let alone serving the Man of God! As far as I was concerned, I was done with that. The pain of being dismissed from church began to rush back. I'm thinking—it's because of the position I was in that caused me to be dismissed from the church. I could not eat after that. I went back into the sanctuary and waited for the next service.

The Lord began to comfort me. He told me that I was in the position at the former church because He put me there. He told me, "You're being placed in this position because I placed you there."

I accepted the assignment; He has graced me to serve senior leadership. Man did not appoint me, God did!

I'm serving on the Bishop's Committee and working in the tape ministry. I'm building relationships within the church. I've been in the ministry for a year and I don't feel connected. I meet with the Bishop and he doesn't have any answers for me. Year two, I meet with the Bishop again and he says that maybe it was just for my healing.

Not only was it for my healing, but it's where God lead me to see my purpose for the world. There were times that I did not see my purpose beyond the four walls. The Lord is so much bigger than the church we attend. It's about His Kingdom and the impact we will make for Him in the world. When I think about Kingdom, I think about the sphere of influence/impact we have among a dying world. We are the light, the answer, the solution to the world's problems.

Question to self...can I be the answer if I don't know who I am in Him. Can I be the solution if I don't look beyond myself? I had to accept and trust that God will do it through me. It's not about ME! When I began to walk in the assurance that He has it covered, He began to reveal the vision He gave me over twelve years ago in a private shut-in. I have the same index card I wrote on when He showed me the vision.

My assignment—solution for the world—is to create a Transitional Housing Program connected with services. The basic idea is an individual will come into the program empty (no housing, no money, no job) and leave out of the program full (house, bank accounts, entrepreneur) and will create opportunities for others.

Yes! This is big! I trust and know that He will bring it to pass.

I've come a long way and feel that I'm on the right path. There are times I wonder why did I have to go through...

- Being dismissed from church

- Failed marriage

- Miscarriage of two children

- Evictions/homelessness/shelters

- Loss of a job

...in order to end up where I am now. Guess what, if I did not go through these things I would not know and trust the Lord as I do now.

I would definitely not be writing my story nor be on my Millionaire/Freedom Journey.

As I look at what the Lord has done in my life, I've often wondered what I would say to myself if I had the opportunity to speak to me at an earlier stage in my life.

The first and foremost advice I would give is, ***"Every woman in the room is just like you."*** For most of my life I've battled with low self-esteem. I always felt when I was in a room that everyone else had more value than me. What they had to say was more important. Through this journey, the Lord let me know that I have value because He created me. There is purpose in me. We all have equal value, but we are all different and unique.

I remember the story my mom told me of my birth. I was slow coming and my mom was having an asthma attack while trying to deliver me. The doctor turned his head and I shot out, and he grabbed my foot before I hit the floor. I don't remember this, but my mom told me I used to wear a foot brace. I believe that nothing happens by happenstance. He did not kill me at birth so now the enemy will attack my value. There's something wrong when you feel you don't measure up. God doesn't create just to create. God is a God of purpose. I'm here to fulfill my destiny and no one else on this earth can accomplish it; it's my assignment and the reason I was brought into the world.

How did I overcome low self-esteem? It was through the Word. The ministry I was now a member of in Lithonia, Georgia showed me through His Word how to accept the gifts and walk them out.

I remember my first class in the School of Ministry was about gifts. My primary gifts are serving and teaching. During the class the facilitator began to say that no gift was more important than the other gift. I said, "What?" (Not realizing I was talking so loud). She repeated it and began to explain how one gift is not more important than another gift is. I know this may not mean a lot to you, but for someone that had been teased about their gift for years—this was an eye opener!

I was at the end of my *Unfamiliar* stage at that time and He wanted me to understand God's Word and to release man's opinion. The thing I feared the most was getting in front of the room. In my opinion I don't speak well and I was afraid of saying the wrong thing. At this stage of my life I facilitate New Member's Class and Small Groups. I trust that He will speak through me and He does!

The second thing that I would tell my younger self is ***"It's your fault for allowing others to use you."*** I was in worship soon after I was dismissed from the church I served in for ten years. As the worship leaders were singing, I closed my eyes and began to ask God why. I felt used and thrown away when I no longer did what was needed. As I held my hands high with tears running down my cheeks the Lord whispered ever so kindly that it was my responsibility not to allow people to use me. He said that people should not, but it's my responsibility to make sure that they don't. This was a news flash for me. No longer could I point the finger at others, but I must deal with why I allowed it to happen.

I'm still an **all-in** individual, but I'm learning that if I notice a shift or that something has changed, I take a step back and wait for further instructions. I'm learning how to give individuals what they want and not what I think they should have or need. A change does not take anything from me or the person who is changing. It's just a change!

My last and final thing I would say to my younger self is to *"Trust God/you're a Millionaire."* This is where I'm headed.

A person who battled with low self-esteem, hated talking in front of people and faces fear on a daily basis wouldn't be pursuing a network marketing profession!

If I did not trust God to build me in the areas that I needed, I would not have pursued this profession. This vehicle will allow me the opportunity to help thousands through the dream/purpose of creating Transitional Housing.

My favorite scripture is Romans 8:28: *And we know that all things work together for good to them that love God, to them who are the called per his purpose.*

All that I am and all that I went through made me who I am today. I would not change anything. I can see a little more clearly now that the good, the bad and the ugly in the hands of the Lord becomes PURPOSE!

We must chase after what He has placed in us. He has placed a dream, a destiny of purpose within us. Our job, responsibility and task is to chase and capture that dream and make it a reality. Regardless of how others see you, you must see yourself in possession of that purpose.

Don't live in the mundane, but live a life of purpose—**ABUNDANCE.** It's never too late to change!

Bio:

Desiree Wicker is a native New Yorker who now resides in Covington, GA. She can be summed up in one word—"Servant." Desiree never knew why she had an overwhelming desire to assist others until it was revealed during a Bible Study lesson on Gifts.

Desiree Wicker has served for over 25 years in the churches she has attended. Her gift of serving has not changed, but it has been enlarged to include the business arena. As an entrepreneur, she serves her team in accomplishing their goals while on her "Millionaire Journey."

Desiree's dream for those she serves within the business arena is financial and time freedom. This freedom will empower them to search, identify, pursue and accomplish their dream(s) that God has placed on the inside of them.

Contact Info:

Desiree J. Wicker
desireewicker@gmail.com

FACE Yourself and You Will Never Quit

Live by *Design* Not by Default

By Richard Price

"You are braver than you believe, smarter than you seem, and stronger than you think."

— Winnie-the-Pooh

(A. A. Milne, Author)

FACE Yourself and You Will Never Quit

By Richard Price

One of the most daunting tasks that man will ever encounter is to come face-to-face with himself. The moment one makes the decision to look inside himself he will have an awakening that will give him the power to endure and never quit.

I grew up in a very competitive and pack-oriented environment where it was feast or famine; you were defined by your circle of influence. And in my case, my personal development was predicated off a broken system, a system built upon falsehoods and limitations. I learned to depend on a faulty system that marginalized my growth and independence. The system I'm referring to is my thought process; it was the vehicle I used to communicate, feel and interpret life. A system with no infrastructure is reckless, and that's exactly what my life was—*reckless*.

This way of thinking and existing had become burdensome and it was time for a radical change; it was time for me to leave who I used to be to become who I wanted to be. It was time for me to put away a dysfunction system I had created that was robbing me of my life. I discovered a pivotal lesson as I turned over a new lease on life. I learned that most people teach what they know but only produce what they are, and for me, I wasn't producing anything. My perception on life was an empty gymnasium, a hollow ground of undirected passion.

Contrary to my own ineptness, I was surrounded by successful family members who seemed to have life by the throat. All around me were talented and gifted athletes and scholars who enjoyed life and excelled at school, yet I struggled in application of the gifts that were within me. My overall expectations were low and I built a fortress around dysfunctional routines. My grandfather used to always encourage me to break routine behavior. I can hear him saying, "Anything done the same way every day is dangerous, Rich. Routine creates comfort, and you should never get comfortable with turbulence. Excuses comfort incapacity."

Boy, was he right! I built routine around problems and fear and I couldn't get out of my own way. I felt like a good seed in bad soil and I grew frustrated and angry because I didn't understand the cards I had been dealt in life. For long periods of time I felt like I had no position to flourish in bad soil. I felt completely out of place and fearful about my future. But as time passed there were small victories along the way, and I learned how to process my feelings while embracing tough times. I learned how to walk through baptism in ordered to be delivered. Unbeknownst to me, life was changing and the scales were falling from my eyes as I was being delivered.

I can recall my first taste of success in school and how amazing it made me feel. It wasn't anything big, but I used to stutter badly. I was very uncomfortable in social settings and I always clinched up if I was under any type of pressure. But on that day I was free; my mind didn't—couldn't—hold me hostage anymore. I remember standing in front of my peers, reading boldly and confidently without missing a beat or stuttering. Wow! What a huge victory that was for me; it was so powerful it created a thirst and a hunger, and I made this feeling my new normal. I learned that you cannot teach a closed mind anything if a person is not hungry to learn.

This was illustrated during the early days of Jesus' pilgrimage. Jesus, the man who could not fail, failed to perform miracles for the non-believers. The key to receiving blessings is faith, to be a believer and walk by faith, not sight. I believe God interrupted my subconscious mind that day in school and reset my thinking. I had an incredible feeling of comfort that re-routed my thinking, and I was free and able to read that day as if I had been reading proficiently and clearly all my life.

For anyone out there who struggles with lack of confidence, God can replenish your every need if you make Him king of your life. I believe God has put in place a process for us all to adhere to and respect. Recklessness and disdain for "process" is dangerous; it often terminates promotion in the process.

I don't believe there is a storm you can't overcome if you remain faithful. So, if you don't like where you are in life right now, remember it's part of the process, these are steps God has ordered in your life. You can't judge your life on where you are right now because in the grand scheme it's just part of the process. TD Jakes said it well when he said, "It's the chaos of time that creates conquests in man." God's strength is made perfect in our weakness!

I later learned that the tests God presents to us is not intended to destroy us but intended to enlighten us. The tests are designed to fortify us so that we may be strong in weak moments. His tests are the tuition we must pay to grow. God said He won't take anything from you He can't replace, and if He can't replace it, He will become it. Through prayer God blesses us with new relationships from some of the most unlikely people.

The oddest relationship I can recall was probably the most memorable one. I can recall many conversations with the neighborhood drunk. He was a sullen man with a distaste for life—so I assumed. He was inebriated half the time and was creating problems the rest of the time. But I remember that one day while I was walking home from school he struck up a conversation with me on the subject of life. How ironic was that? A man who had appeared to have given up on life decided to share his perspective on life. I remember him telling me how good life is and the moment you stop respecting life, life will turn on you and you will live in perpetual pain. I was stunned by what he said to me and how much sense it made. I was thinking to myself, what an unlikely source to be giving a history lesson of life, but because of who it came from I was even more attracted to his jargon.

Isn't it funny how you can find a gem anywhere if you look for it? I can't count how many times I walked past this man, prejudging him and feeling sorry for him. TD Jakes was right when he said, "If you die over who you have met, you will miss out on who you are going to meet." Anyways, I was partial to my secret friend and he became a significant source in my maturation process. I grew to depend on him for nourishment. I recall him saying, "Rich, you are awesome, young brother; you can do what you set your mind to do if you want it bad enough." For a while it was very hard for me to process the positive and encouraging words without feeling hoodwinked. I mean his words were full of confirmation yet he had not lived by his own words.

It took me a long time to understand what he saw in me that I didn't see in myself. I realized that he was starving my doubts by strengthening my faith. He made me believe that I didn't lack aptitude, I lacked faith and confidence. He explained to me that a lack of faith and confidence creates a cavity to fill. I remember him telling me that in life you are either supplying or creating a demand for something. Why not supply and create a demand for something you believe in?

Hello! That went way over my head: I wasn't ready for that. As I reflect back on some of those conversations, they were some of the most enriching and powerful moments of my life. My greatest regret was not applying many of those insightful principles earlier in my life and recognizing that God will sometimes send people you don't even recognize to bless you. I wish I knew if he was still living because I owe him a special thanks.

Listen to me, God hears your cries for help, but you have to be aware of whom he's sending your way to bless you. I believe it is the things that God reveals to us during our journey that make us who we are. I have also learned that the race in not given to the swift, it's given to the one who can endure the longest.

The stark reality is all we have in life is NOW. Of course, we can't frame everything in a *do it right now* mentality. Some things are developed over time. Over time I began to find the courage within myself to encourage myself to never quit.

I soon came to realize that all the things that I was fearful of were a manifestation of what was to become of my life. And for those of you who are running from your destiny, it's time to stop and confront your fears because if you are going through a battle it's because you're building something special.

Isaiah 54: 16-17 "I have created the blacksmith who fans the coals beneath the forge and make the <u>weapons of destruction</u>. NO weapon formed against you shall prosper." **Translation: There shall be no fears within; there shall be no fighting without. The emphasis of an open heart creates a cavity for God to fill, but a closed mind never receives anything.**

Why do people quit? They have no idea that they can win. The forces around them and that surround them have told them that they don't quite cut it. They don't have the passion to identify what they were born to do. They have never taken an inventory of what's happening in their own life to figure out what they want to happen in that same life.

In many cases, they are not honest with themselves about the success or failures that they've experienced. Oftentimes, the successes were just blown off as mere coincidence and the failures were labeled as the norm. Furthermore, they have not identified others that are succeeding in the manner or in the direction that they would like to. They don't have something or someone bigger than themselves to lean on and to prop them up. They haven't sold themselves on themselves. Finally, their circle of influence influences them in the wrong way. They don't have an accountability coach. They look at life as a trial and error of events with no positive focus. They are restricted by their own barriers that they have created and placed on their life, and they don't understand how to begin rescuing themselves.

As I began to scale up to success and stop the starting and failing syndrome that I had become accustomed to, I began that to realize that success is a process, and anyone who gets there too soon oftentimes don't have the aptitude to sustain it. I also discovered that the difference between myself and those I admire is their perception on life. I realized that if you are disciplined in your perspective you will be victorious with your outcomes. Freedom is about destiny and purpose and finding out who you are and where you fit in while being authentic. This is living by design and not by default, but unfortunately for many people the starting process is the same as the breaking point. Most times people bring their past into the future and the future just becomes a replay of that past.

For years, I condemned myself as a failure because I was not producing anything satisfactory. My confidence was shaky, my perception on life was unclear, and I was afraid to grow wings and unfortunately I sabotaged my vision. It takes a lot of work to redevelop your thinking and to enjoy a resurrected thought life. Life teaches you a lot about yourself if you are conscious and understand that your thinking must align with your expectations. When your thinking is clear, expected results follow enabling you to live with purpose.

It is in not understanding the possibilities that the possible becomes impossible. People quit due to buying into the reality of their yesterday instead of looking to the possibility of their tomorrow. We have a natural inclination to quit. To continue toward a target or mark or goal requires that we become a new believer; we have to be delivered based on what we see in the future, not what we are experiencing in our present. The Bible says that at some point in our lives "We all will have a cross to bear which defines the moment in life where we will meet despair face–to–face, and we will have to bow down, calling on Jesus to save or intervene on our behalf."

I had to be coached to a new commitment. Coaching allowed me to help me see myself winning. My coaches allowed me to borrow their belief in me. I believe they saw me achieving much better and doing much better than the reality I was experiencing.

Coaching allows you to have someone other than yourself to help you succeed. It's not their job to do the work for you; it's their job to let you know that you are capable, you are worthy and you have the ability to reach the dreams that you set for yourself.

As you watch others do what you want to do, they become the role models that you should follow. I had quit on many things until I discovered some painful truths—the pain of failing, the pain of quitting, the pain of unfulfilled dreams. The most important lesson that I learned is *don't fool yourself.*

Don't fall for the trick of believing that you're winning, when you know that you're losing. Quitting is a loser's game. You should see how different it could be if you were willing to pursue the things that you actually wanted to achieve. That's what facing yourself is about. You see, if you are not willing to face the guy in the mirror you will never know who you can truly be. I'm still learning that your greatest failure in life always precedes your greatest success.

In truth, you must have the same faith in your failures as you do in your success if you intend to grow. It all revolves around having a solid foundation, a foundation you are secure with and is your bedrock. Now for many, it's quite possible that your foundation was laid for you. Here is the good news. God has ordered your steps and with His help you can lay a new foundation for your life built on faith and provision. So even if your blueprint has been poured for you, you control your destiny, because what's restricting is not around you, it's in you. The key is to acknowledge the controllable things in your life and stop blaming outside stuff for inside turmoil. That's where many of us find ourselves...living dead. I began to ask the hard questions of myself and face myself, and I found several components necessary in facing myself, to accept myself, the first of which was commitment.

I'm learning to this day that you can't inspire people to follow your own lack of commitment. Most people follow what they admire and anything that you desire to do requires a full commitment because you can't conquer what you are not committed to.

This was really hard in the beginning but it became the most powerful force that began to change my life for the better. It taught me to be intentional about what I wanted to do. And if you want to succeed and to win and finally face yourself, that intentionality must be inbred into your DNA.

Many wrongs can be made right, but only if they are turned into a learning opportunity. All the wrong and the negative results should not cause us to beat ourselves up and feel that we failed; instead, it should be an opportunity for us to learn how to move forward to the successes we desire.

Every obstacle is an opportunity to win. Opportunity is found in opposition, but you must be planted in something much bigger than yourself. We often think that oppositional obstacles are meant for our demise but it's meant for innovation and growth. However, the key to discovering that the opposition is merely opportunities in disguise depends on your perspective. If your perspective is right, you can create wining opportunities out of losing opportunities. You must ask yourself why you want to win. And also, why you're willing to quit.

One of the great kings of the Bible, King David, illustrated this when faced with daunting opposition, and he rose to the occasion. David, a young boy, stood up and offered to face Goliath, a menacing warrior known for combat. David, a sheepherder, rose to the occasion and remembered what God had done for him when he defeated the

Lion and the Bear. David's faith was so deep that he used his faith to stand up against this mighty giant, and he saw an opportunity where others saw defeat in the opposition. David, who was mocked by the champion and by his own brothers, stood firm and saw an opportunity to be victorious despite the odds. David called on his faith and chose impracticality to defeat Goliath. The weapon that is used against many of us is fear and doubt, but David went against the grain and stepped out on faith and became one of the greatest men of the Bible.

Our stories aren't that different in application from those (characters) in the Bible because we will all face giants throughout our life. The opposition in your life may feel so great and unbeatable, but you can and will defeat your Goliath. Remember, you can't conquer what you are afraid of, and in any area of your life that you expect more than you invest, giants exist. The opposition is not really real. Opposition is merely the birthing pains that lead to the birth of our dreams and desires. Every opposition has an opportunity within it. It is our will to see the success that we're seeking. We must embrace the opposition and find a mission in it.

The question is, do we want it bad enough? And are we willing to go through perpetual discomfort to achieve greatness. D. H. Howard said it best when he said, "If the dream is big enough we will find the courage and strength to move toward it, in spite of, because of, that opposition."

What is needed to move on is to get rid of the mindset of where you have been and focus on where you want to go. It's all about constantly discovering what is inside of you. This requires getting a stronger perspective on your individual situation to be able to defeat the giants in your life. Remember, this is all part of God's plan for you to grow in adversity, finding your purpose and allowing it to transcend your life where passion ebbs and flows.

You must sell yourself on yourself that you will make it and that everything you are and want to be is already in you. The Bible states that everything you are going to be must come from the heart because out of the heart flows the issues of life. I believe that our destiny is already in us, but we must be willing to work out our gifts and abilities. Time has taught me the moment you hand over your selfishness, God will provide you purpose and influence.

In conclusion, you must monitor your doubts and fears while aligning your gifts to match your purpose. The greatest expression is not in the destination, it's in the process, and it's in who you are becoming along the way. Robert Ruth said it best when he said, "It's not what you don't have, it's what you think you need to be successful and happy in life."

Bio:

My name is Rich Price and I'm from Cleveland, Ohio but I reside in Michigan. I'm married with four different but independent children whom make my life worthwhile. I work in the higher education sector as a master senior recruiter/expert relationship advisor as well as an inspiring speaker. I have two master degrees: Master of Business Administration with a concentration in Marketing and Master of Public Administration Political Science.

I would like to use my story and passion to educate and serve others and to build a legacy that my children can carry on. I'm in the business of fertilizing and nourishing acorns and watching them blossom into massive oak trees. We are the acorn of an oak tree, and with the right mentoring, coaching and love, we can become the oak tree God has called us to be.

"Life is a fight for territory. Once you stop fighting for what you want, what you don't want will automatically take over" - Les Brown

Contact info: richp254@gmail.com

I Lost SIGHT but Never VISION

Live by *Design* Not by Default

By Pamela Robinson

"The only thing worse than being blind is having sight and no vision."

— Helen Keller

I Lost SIGHT but Never VISION
By: Pamela Robinson

All too often we rely on sight and forget about the value of vision. I tend to think of sight as strategies, insights, goals, habits and tactics. All of them are designed to get us from one point to the other, to see what we can have, what we can be, what we're striving for. But more important than sight is vision.

After a very successful high school basketball career I was recruited to several places and ended up playing at several different universities, some by choice, some by circumstance. I was outside playing a pickup game of basketball with some friends when I noticed that my vision was a little blurry. It bothered me enough that I went to the hospital. They just suggested that I go to an eye doctor or ophthalmologist. I guess hindsight is more important than insight, because I should have been given a thorough examination.

The next day my vision was worse, and I went to the eye doctor. After using all the modern tools and techniques they announced that there were no problems and that I was okay, but clearly, I was not. The next morning I woke up and my vision was much blurrier and much worse. My mom and I decided to go see a specialist to get a second opinion. As we got ready to leave, I lost all sight in my left eye. My eye was open like a window, but all I saw was darkness.

I'm not one to engage in panic. Needless to say that with no visual sight in my eye, I was a bit concerned. So my mother and I decided to go to another hospital. They ordered tests, which included several MRIs and CAT scans. It was discovered that there was a lesion on my brain. Additionally, they even did a spinal tap, which involves putting a needle in my spine to pull out fluid. I'm not going to say that is a risky procedure, but it is difficult and painful at best.

After these tests were performed, they transported me back to my room in a wheelchair. As an athlete, I've always looked upon wheelchairs as a disability that made me feel restricted, but I guess they were necessary to prevent malpractice concerns for the doctor.

My family was there and all of us anxiously awaited the results. The results came back and indicated optic neuritis, which is a precursor to multiple sclerosis. MS—who would have ever thought it? My only concern was, "Doc, can I still play; can I continue to do well and pursue my career and my degree?"

The doctor gave an emphatic **"sure,"** but he suggested that there may be side effects to the medications, such as seizures and heart problems that were not guaranteed, but the possibility was always there.

I had a different path, a different focus, and a different direction that I wanted to proceed in. I didn't have time to take on their truth regarding my life. I had a vision for what I wanted my life to be, and it didn't include being an invalid or being sick or being disabled.

They began a steroid-based treatment and it began working. I was not willing to surrender to the facts for their diagnosis. I had a different protocol for healing, which was faith-based, holistic in the mindset. This meant I was willing to focus on the body attacking itself and to change the paradigm to what I believed was more currently true and correct about my reality. This may not have been psychologically the best health decision, but it was when I made it. I engaged in the denial of reality and acceptance to move forward.

Life has many gray areas. Even while feeling isolated I heard other people with similar issues and they were declaring themselves healed. Although the declaration of healing produces a great feeling, the symptoms were still present nonetheless. Many of the holistic practitioners that I consulted had conflicting viewpoints on that reality.

Several suggested that I acknowledge the negative reality and begin focusing on the positive alternative. Others suggested that I just ignore the reality and instead only focus on the alternative. My only concern was that I wanted to play in college, and to play professionally, and all the people involved in this holistic process knew that.

Prior to the diagnosis of MS I had very little, if any, playing time. I questioned my former coach about it; he was not honest with me and suggested that I knew what the reasons were. After much introspection and indecision, I decided to sever the relationship. I transferred from that college and ended up at Old Westbury in Hicksville, New York. I was able to make the team and as I began practice, I realized that my sight really affected my ability to play.

I give you that background to bring you up to snuff to where I am today in my life and what happened to bring me to that point. The next two years I played with an intensity beyond which I've ever played before. I began to realize many of my dreams. I played at Old Westbury with many debilitating problems in my health. The eye issues were there, and I had to compensate for the many issues it produced. My depth perception was affected greatly. Many times, I would either overshoot or undershoot because I thought the hoop was closer or further than what it was. Or I would reach to receive a pass that hadn't quite made it to me yet and would jam my fingers and thumbs. This caused me to play with my thumbs wrapped in tape because I was continually jamming them.

I hid these concerns from my teammates early on because I didn't want to have an excuse or to use that as an excuse for not playing at my best. The coaches were aware and I continued to play and excel by playing with an intensity that was unlike how I had played in previous schools. I wanted now to reach the goal that I had on the inside.

All of that led to a mantra that I subscribed to in life which is about VISION. And as I look at the word *vision,* I began to see the story of my life unfold before my very eyes. Through the trials and tribulations of life, I navigated them as best as I could. From school to school, from wellness to sickness, from dreams realized to dreams deferred, these are some of the paths I navigated. Sometimes we get curve balls thrown at us. Sometimes we are doing the throwing. Such is the bitter and sweet of victory. Victory is the first part of my mantra of VISION.

Victory

Victory is not always the bigger picture. The victory is in the smaller details. I did what I needed to do today. Each victory has a beginning and an end, but more importantly, the victory is in between. My victory started in the hospital with the question, **"Can I still play?"**

That thought plagued me throughout the journey. So many things seemed to put themselves in my path. These things in my path could have been distractions or simply a part of the path toward victory. I've looked at the many victories that I have achieved, and I know that victory starts with the small battles. I was named an honorable mention All-American basketball player for my short two-year career at Old Westbury, but just being able to get on the court was a victory. Being able to adapt to the game when in reality I was facing so many obstacles was a victory. Being able to get close to the potential that I knew was inside of me was a victory. That is what victory meant to me. So, victory became the avenue from which I viewed life.

Victory is not some significant event at some far-off time. Victory is winning every day. Victory is waking up in the morning when you're tired, frustrated and feeling defeated. Victory is overcoming the obstacles the life puts along the way one by one. Victory is not always the significant battle or the incredible war won;

victory is winning the small battles along the way. Victory for me was just being able to play, being able to overcome and adjust to the difficulty of my situation.

Many of you are facing significant battles in your life. Being able to even compete at the level necessary to win is a victory. Do not ignore the small victories and act as if they are insignificant. The many victories along the way lead to the big victory at the end. To know that you're victorious means that you've overcome battle after battle, test after test, circumstance and situation after circumstance and situation. It means that you were willing to keep on though the odds were against you. Victory means whenever it seemed impossible and everyone else counted you out, you thrived anyway. Victory is looking at the insignificant and realizing its significance.

For me victory was being able to get on the court every night, being able to push myself beyond the limit. Victory for me was making a shot when I couldn't clearly see the basket. Victory for me was all these incidental seemingly insignificant things that led up to the larger picture of winning and winning at all costs. Victory is not the big picture:

victory is everything that makes the picture possible.

Integrity

The **I** in **VISION** means **Integrity**.

Integrity has many meanings, but it all boils down to transparency. Transparency is being open and not hiding your motives or agenda. Upon my initial diagnosis, I felt it best to not share it with my teammates. The coaches and staff were well aware and worked with me. Intentional accountability requires that you are open and operate on a focused intent to accomplish a specific goal. There was a rash of reasons why I chose not to let my teammates know that I was going through a medical crisis. Primarily, I didn't want them to feel sorry for me or feel that I was incapable of handling pressure.

As the captain of the team I was playing at a high-level already. When I realized that I was operating from a position of weakness and not my usual strength, I tried to compensate by overcompensating. I worked hard, and even that is an understatement. Everyone on the team was working hard, so even if I worked less we would've still been at a championship caliber. I knew I had to step up unless I got injured in a physical way.

Integrity is character personified, accountability of what was happening regardless of the outcome. Integrity required that I operate at the optimum level. If others saw me sitting back, not giving it my all, they would've felt compelled to, or at least inclined to operate at a level less than their best, or they would have judged me as being incapable of being a captain. I realized that the medical issue was in me but I was not in it. I had control over it and everything that was involved with it. For me integrity meant going beyond what others saw in me and doing what I saw in myself. Pushing myself to limits that I didn't even know existed.

At one point I was playing in an intense game and twisted my ankle and had to be carried off the court. The high level of intensity and integrity within me caused me get it taped it up quickly so I could get up and get back in the game. Life is about staying in the game, pushing yourself past the limits that others have imposed on you. Limits are an illusion to you if you operate from a position of integrity, trying to do better than your best. Perfection is the bane of excellence. Perfection says that you want to do it, but it is beyond possibility. Excellence says that you can do it to the best of your ability. Integrity is what pushes you to be your best.

It has been said that integrity is doing your best even when nobody is watching. I took that to heart. I was able to see beyond what was seen. In my vision for victory, integrity became the lamp unto my feet. Integrity became the weapon that I used to win the war or at least the battle. As long as I knew that I was doing all I could do, that was all I was willing to do, able to do, and I would do my best.

Security

While integrity was a lamp leading me, guiding and lighting my way, security was what kept me along the path. The **S** in **VISION** stands for **Security**. Security talks about safety versus success. I went a holistic route versus the traditional route to handle my medical issue. Security said that you had to be safe, that your body had to have a chance to heal in order to be able to be productive. The inner voice said "don't push so hard, keep yourself safe and secure, you don't have to work so hard. Your safety and health is more important than the team." For me security went beyond just my selfish needs and eclipsed the concept that winning is the ultimate thing.

The safe route would have been to give the appearance of pushing while reserving myself and securing my health. Instead, I went beyond that. Sure, I took the proper measures to preserve and prepare myself, but I decided to go further. At the end of a practice, sometimes I would stay in the gym and take 1000 jump shots to compensate for my vision impairment. Sometimes I would go to my local youth center and shoot and practice more there. If that place was closed, sometimes I would go out in the neighborhood and simply dribble the ball through the streets of my neighborhood. Additionally, I watched film after film, analyzing myself and how I was playing. That, relentless work ethic provided security and led me to a more secure future.

I saw the necessity to work on and overcome my deficiencies so that they would not be seen. I felt that it was emotionally unsafe for me to give into the disease. My mantra and philosophy has always been to live full and die empty. Living full means to give it all that you have so that when you are finished, you have nothing else left to give.

I began to play a different dialogue in my mind. There are many gray areas that people face in their lives. The hard black-and-white areas are the extremes that exist for everyone. Most people live in that gray area, that nebulous world of not knowing. I felt it was time to say something else or shut up.

In other words, shut up the voices in my mind telling me to play it safe and not get the full security that winning brings. I had begun to operate at that unconscious level for so long that I was no longer conscious of the results that spoke for themselves. The results led to my new identity.

Identity

The second **I** in **VISION** stands for **Identity**. As captain of the team I was not a vocal leader; my actions spoke louder than my words. My identity was one that was not to be average; I was striving for excellence. During my journey, a newspaper interviewed me and watched me. Once they finished their article, there eventually appeared a full-page article of me in *Newsday*; they titled it "One Tough Competitor."

That was an **ID** that others saw based on what I was doing. I embraced the struggle. For me being tough meant just toughing it out. As I played most of that year with bandaged fingers and thumbs due to not being able to adequately assess the proximity of the ball, I began to shape a new **ID**. The toughness that others saw in me was me being tough on myself. Not allowing myself to quit or give mediocre or average performance.

My identity was shaped every day and it was not easy. I was demanding more of myself. And the more I asked of myself the more my wonderful teammates and coaches recognized and respected me for it. Thus, I will be the first woman being inducted into The Sports Hall of Fame at SUNY Old Westbury. My **ID** is not the end of the story, it's just a beginning. Legacies are formed when you push yourself beyond the perceived limits being imposed on you. The Hall of Fame was not the fame I was seeking but a result of having an identity that I could be proud of.

Accolades are honorable but the dream, the **ID** for me, was to Go Pro. Your identity is shaped by every moment that you step onto the court of life, every moment that you take that shot. Your **ID** is determined by whether or not you're willing to shape the identity based on your efforts and your dream. That identity leads to opportunity.

Opportunity

The **O** in **VISION** stands for **Opportunity**. I took advantage of every opportunity presented to me. Many times, I had to create opportunities from high school to college to my current career. Every day I wake up is an opportunity, another chance to make another move forward. When I received that call to go and play college ball in South Carolina, that was an opportunity. I could've passed it up or taken advantage of it. I chose to take advantage. The truth is indeed stranger than fiction. Every small opportunity leads to a larger opportunity. Each opportunity presents itself as another chance at victory and legacy.

As I was trying to reconstruct my college ball career after a two-year layoff, I began applying for financial aid. I was denied time and time again because the household income that my mother created was beyond the threshold of what I was allowed under the financial threshold. I was on my own at the time. I began saving and doing everything possible to take advantage of another opportunity to get back in the game.

In order to take advantage of the opportunities that were presenting themselves to me I was fortunate enough to have friends in the airline industry who allowed me to use buddy passes. I flew all over the country to look at opportunities. One opportunity that presented itself was for a chance to play in Arizona. I flew out and was hoping for that scholarship. The truth be told I was not in shape and not really ready for the opportunity, but I tried all the same. As I tried out, the coach looked at me and said, "You look like you used to be able to play."

That was a huge slap in the face as doors begin to close, but they led to new doors being opened. They looked to bypass potential and I felt as if I was hindered by closed doors from the past. Another coach in Oklahoma gave me an opportunity, stating, "If you can beat me one on one I will give you the scholarship." I played my heart out in that one-on-one game against the coach and I lost. I lost the scholarship as well.

We often look at those closed doors as lack of opportunity; for me it just led to more focus in such an intense desire that I forced myself to take advantage of new opportunities. Often, we have harsh closures. People don't see the potential in us that we see in ourselves. I played hurt but I moved forward nonetheless. The law of probability and opportunity says something is waiting for you every day. My story didn't end there, as I sought other opportunities and finally prevailed.

Notoriety

The **N** in **VISION** means **Notoriety**. I didn't see myself aligned for notoriety; in fact, I wasn't looking for it at all. I was led to speak motivationally and that was never really something that was within me. After the article appeared I was given opportunity after opportunity to speak, but I struggled within because of the spotlight.

It's lonely at the top and I have always been concerned with connecting with people. At the same time, I wanted to achieve my goals and that would require climbing higher. Many people don't want to climb, which leaves the bottom entirely too crowded. There are reasons why mountains have peaks, because only a few will ever try to climb up them. Despite knowing this, I craved connection and feared that I would lose connection to my teammates and myself, as well as to my family. As I reached the second year of that season I reached the thousand-point mark—I was doing what I always dreamed of doing. But I struggled with success. Notoriety is not what I chased, but it chased me.

Just seeking my goals when I got to SUNY Old Westbury, was all I wanted to do. All I wanted was to reach my goals. I received a paradigm of acceptance. I had been self-sabotaging myself on some level—I was afraid of climbing too high. The higher you elevate—whether you are climbing or on a plane—there is less air the higher you go. Somehow, regardless of that, I was able to breathe and thrive due to focus. I was focused on something beyond just the season, beyond just the college. I was focused on *going pro*. The best spotlight is to have the light shine within you so bright that you can see yourself.

Often, we are not comfortable with the spotlight that others shine on us, so we try to dim the light. Vision means being able to shine the light on the inside so that you'll be able to see what you're seeking. As I learned the necessity to share my story with the world I realized that I was learning from everyone. Everyone has a story that connects us.

As I was losing sight, I always kept the vision of victory—the vision of being able to move forward and achieve and accomplish all the dreams, goals, desires and hopes within me.

As I end this chapter I share that with you as well. It's time for you to have new vision. A VISION to not lose sight of the fact that your yesterdays have lit your path to new and better tomorrows—tomorrows that begin every day you wake up and touch the ground. Every day that you can look forward to seeing your VISION become a reality. Nothing can stop you unless you allow it to. Nothing can prevent you from reaching the success that you desire unless your desire is not to go higher.

The road to success is paved with bumps and detours, distractions and disappointments. It's up to you to keep your sight on the vision. And if things happen to make the vision become foggy, and you lose sight of it, remember, sight is only what you see on the outside. VISION is on the inside.

Bio:

Pamela Robinson is a LIGHT speaker and LIGHT coach. LIGHT = **Lifting-Inspiring-Guiding-Helping-Transforming**. Pam encourages people to find their own LIGHT and move toward illuminating the lives of others. She found her calling through her diagnosis of multiple sclerosis back in 2007.

Since that time, she has completed two degrees while having a Hall of Fame basketball career at SUNY Old Westbury. She also had a short stint professionally through signing with various smaller teams in the U.S. Pamela will be inducted in the SUNY Old Westbury's Sports Hall of Fame in 2017.

She has decided to live a life that is dedicated to helping others look inside themselves and move forward. Through examining your own mind, and how you perceive the world, she believes that human potential is limitless and is something we all can know by looking inside ourselves.

Contact info:

Instagram : pamela _robinson24
Twitter: Pamela Robinson or
TheOneWhoWokeUp

Pamela Robinson on Facebook:
pamela.robinson24@gmail.com

pamela.robinson24@gmail

Live Life by Design Not by Default

Live by
Design
Not by Default

By Dr. Kim Ladson

"The man who has no imagination has no wings."

— Muhammad Ali

Live Life by Design Not by Default
By Dr. Kim Ladson

To reach new destinations in life, you should design a blueprint for getting there. I heard the great motivational speaker, Les Brown once say that "Life is a fight for territory, and if you don't fight for what you want, what you don't want will automatically take over."

That statement was probably the most important statement that I have ever heard, read, or seen because it helped me change my view on life. As a young girl, I had dreams of becoming successful. I didn't at first know what I wanted to be successful in. I just knew I wanted to make a lot of money. I grew up in the projects and my days and nights were filled with signs of lack and poverty; yet, I knew inside that that wasn't me. Somehow, I knew that I was different from the environment that I was in. Physically, I was in lack, but lack was not in me. I had dreams. There was more in me; I just didn't know how to get to it. Later on in life I found my passion for speaking, for training, and for writing. I wanted to become a world-renowned speaker, a best-selling author, and a world-class trainer, but more than anything else, I wanted to help people become greater versions of themselves. I had no idea then that regardless of what my dreams were, for me to live them, I had to fight.

I had to fight through the projects, through the graffiti-filled walls, through the urine-smelling elevators, through the drug dealers, through the drunken people on the corners, through the welfare lines, and through the empty refrigerators, and I had to grab hold to the vision I had inside of me. A vision that said I could do, be, and experience more in my life. Sometimes you have to look at your circumstances and say, regardless of what I see, there is greater in me and there is greater for me. I don't know your name, I don't know where you are, and I don't know what you are going through in your life right now, but can I stop for a moment to tell you that there is *Greater* in you and there is *Greater* for you. *Fight for it.*

You see, there is a fight in life that we all are in. It is the fight to live your best life, the fight to experience your dreams, and the fight to walk in the destiny and purpose you were called to. Many people have dreams and goals, yet many of them don't fight for the right to achieve them. When you don't fight for what you want in life, you will get what you don't want. Many people are not happy with where they are in life. They don't like what they see. They don't like what they have. They don't like what they are experiencing. Yet, where we are in life, what we have, and where we are going, are results of the decisions we have made. Sometimes we just let life happen. We go along and let the day happen to us instead of making the day happen for us. When we do that, we decide not to fight.

Even if you don't decide, you've made a decision. Your non-decision is a decision. That decision determines the outcome of your life. Many people would rather acquiesce to indifference, and not put forth the effort or the struggle to achieve and win. In other words, many people are unwilling to confront or to fight for a future that they alone can design. Instead, by default, they find themselves living a life that they haven't chosen.

In essence, it's necessary to shape, to mold, and to design the destiny that you desire. Deciding not to do something is a decision to do nothing. Ultimately, we all reap the results of our decisions. Not to study is to fail, not to diet is to stay fat, not to invest in your marriage or in yourself means that you're not going forward. Instead you are really going backwards. While writing this book, I was asked, "What's the meaning of life to you?" As I thought about the question, I realized that between life and death is this thing called **why.** Life is about discovering your why, developing your why, and living your why. We all have a **why**, a reason for being here, and finding out what that **why** is, living it, and making a difference with it, is life to me. Life is about doing and living the life that God created for you to live.

Ultimately, we're here to make the world a better place, and to achieve significance. The meaning of life is the ability to make the world a better place to live in, to leave your fingerprint, and to impact the lives of others with the gifts and talents God has placed in you.

Benjamin Franklin said that many people die at the age of twenty-five but aren't buried until they are seventy-five. They die at twenty-five because that is when they stop living, dreaming, and fighting for what they want in life. They exist as empty zombielike shells that walk around in life wondering why their passion and purposes aren't being fulfilled.

Not doing the things that you're passionate about, that you're yearning for, is what causes not only frustration but also stagnation. Not living out dreams, not being happy is where most people find themselves. Over 85% of people polled were not happy with their current work. Many people work a job just to make a living, just to make money. But sadly, money doesn't answer the yearning, the passion you have inside for significance and importance.

I've often told a story about my grandmother; she was my rock, the source of my foundation. When she passed, I was devastated. She raised me to be a powerful strong young lady. She was all I had once both of my parents were deceased. She was short in statue, but tall in faith. There was not a day that passed by that I didn't see her pray. She showed me how to beat the odds through faith. She was the one who told me not to look at what I see, but to only see what I believed.

As a young girl, I shared with my grandmother my dreams of being successful. She pulled me aside and looked me in my eyes with conviction and certainty and said, "You can be whatever you want to be, baby." I believed her. "Your way out is through faith and through education," she said.

She pushed me to study and to do well in school, and that I did. I graduated at the top of my class. I received a five-year grant to go to Long Island University. I was excited; I knew that I was destined for success. My freshman year in school went extremely well. I had a 4.0 grade point average each semester. I was on the dean's list. Because of my passion to make a difference, I ran for freshman council, and I won. I was amazed. It was the most exciting part of my life. There was no doubt in my mind that I was winning in life.

I entered my second year, optimistic and energetic about my future. It started off just as well as my freshman year. I maintained my 4.0 average and my involvement in the school. Then one day after school, I received a call to come home right away.

When I entered the house, I saw faces filled with tears and anguish.

"What happened?" I yelled. "What happened?" My aunt grabbed me and said, "Grand Mommy passed away. She died in her sleep."

I couldn't believe it. Not my grandmother. She was my rock, my foundation. She can't be dead, I thought. Instantly, I was afraid, bewildered and alone. It was a reality that I had to face. My grandmother was gone. I found myself in college without my support system, without my foundation and without my strength. I couldn't continue. I had to drop out. I had nowhere to live. I had no one to support me. I had to survive on my own. This young lady had to grow up quickly.

Sometimes life will hit you with an unexpected occurrence. You may lose a loved one, a relationship, a home, a job, and some finances. These are all things in life that we must fight through. This was a devastating moment for me because my grandmother always told me that my success was attached to my education, so when I dropped out, I felt like I was dropping out of my future, out of my success, and out of my dreams.

I struggled for a while, doing my best to keep my head above water. I stopped chasing dreams and I began chasing money. I took whatever job would pay me the most money. I was working, but I wasn't happy. My dreams continued speaking to me, whispering in my spirit. It wasn't until later that I realized that the most powerful ingredient my grandmother taught me was faith—the power of belief. That faith didn't die; it was still in me. I had power to believe. I remember that she told me not to look at what I see, but to only see what I believed.

I began to fight and I began to see my dreams. Possibilities, hope, and ideas began to live in me, and I began to take steps toward the things I wanted in life. I went back to school in the evening to get my degree. I continued my education to obtain my graduate degree. I continued day by day to work on myself to build my dreams. Even today, I continue to work on myself and my dreams.

We were made to thrive and not just survive. To thrive means that you have more joy. More fullness. More peace. You can work to just pay the bills and have a weekend of leisure, but true success is to go beyond the average and doing the things that you were created to do.

I see so many people in a zombielike cycle. They are not happy with their life. They have gotten caught up in just going through the formalities of life. They find themselves at a point of unknown purpose and have no idea of God's purpose for their lives. We all have responsibilities like bills, family and taking care of minimal things. Yet, there is something inside of us all that seeks greater expression and greater stations in life.

The zombie state becomes so commonplace, and most people that define themselves feel it's normal. It's not normal. Normal is that cause, that calling, that yearning, and that burning desire that says, *"There is more."* Prayer is talking to God. Intuition is God talking to us. God is saying there is more.

When we feel a desire and/or a pulling for more, that is usually God telling us that we can be, do, and have more. It may not be an overnight completion, but it doesn't have to take a lifetime either. There is a path to your dreams and it starts with you mapping out a plan to go down that path.

If you are not happy with where you are in life, you should set an exit date.

The planning of that exit is the designing of your life, and when you design your life, opportunities will open for you. It is not easy to just up and leave places in our lives. We have jobs, careers, relationships, and stations in life that we are connected to, and it is not easy just to leave, but at the same time it is not easy to stay. It takes time, but it starts with you making a decision. You have a right to live the life you imagine. Wherever you are in life, make the decision that you will go after the *more* you desire.

It becomes overwhelming to see where we are and understand that we may have to start all over in order to reach our dreams and goals. What I've learned in life is that we don't have to start over. We can just start from where we are and start chronicling the path to where we should be and want to be. There is a Japanese proverb that says, ***a journey of 1000 miles begins with one step.*** It means getting in the car and putting it into gear and going forward toward that dream.

It doesn't have to take a lifetime; it's possible now! We can chronicle our age, education, bank account or any number of things that will prevent us from achieving the dream and reaching that goal. But if we have the audacity to dream it, God gives us the audacity to fulfill that dream. You can't have what you don't go after. We must do something different to have something different. Surround yourself with different people that have different ways of thinking and take different actions.

Clarity is the first step toward the process. Many of us are stuck at start and that's due to a lack of clarity. The question becomes, how do you fight to design your destiny? It starts with asking some very personal and powerful questions.

Who am I?

What do I want?

What do I want to do?

Where do I want to go?

What do I need to do to do it?

What type of life do I want to live?

I discovered that it's all about discovering your **why**. And part of your **why** is to discover who's going in the same direction that you want to go. You see, if you want to get to where you want to get to, you could go fast by yourself but you can get there further and faster when you surround yourself with people that are going in that same direction. People are willing to help you if you're willing to reach out and ask and receive it once it is presented to you. Living the designed life is about changing and challenging yourself. It will take five significant steps to achieve success that is changing and challenging.

1. What you think

2. What you see

3. What you say

4. What you do

5. What you believe

When we are designing our lives and creating our dreams, we must think, see, say, do, and believe the life that we imagine. We must see ourselves doing the things we want to do, living the life we want to have, and becoming the person we want to become. The things we need to change in our life are already inside us. We must tap into the power that is in us.

The first step requires that we *do the first step*. Many people, when it comes to their dreams tell themselves, **Someday I'll**...Someday I'll write that book, someday I'll take that trip, someday I'll go back to school. The sad truth is there is no place call someday. You must begin and begin now. Someday is not on any calendar of the week, success is in small steps taken in the present, in the now. Small steps connect us toward moving toward a dream or goal. Small steps separate us from those who major in the minors from those who do what they want to do. The difference is doing.

It takes jumping into that design that you created. It doesn't require that you be smarter or better, just that you do it, that you design it and do it. The toughest thing is believing that we can do it. But the fact that you can dream it is a sign that you can do it. It will not be easy, but it will be possible.

And yes, life comes with unexpected storms. Storms that disrupt your day. Storms that sometimes can be a disaster in your day. You may be knocked down as part of the process. Each storm, each knockdown carries with it, within it, a lesson to be learned. The storms are not the enemy; they are your friends. The storms bring us the wisdom to win.

That storm may be a hurting, a crying, and a regrouping. The question you must ask yourself is, "What did I learn?" You must evaluate the experience and realize that whether you were right or wrong, somehow you learned, and it helps you to get to the next level that you were designed to be.

Know that each day you may experience new issues, but in reality, they are the same issues, just with new faces and new names. All experiences come to teach us and bring the best out of us. We must learn that life is not our enemy, but a friend. Everyday we're going to learn something new that will help us fight to get through. We must fight. We fight by getting up when we are knocked down, by moving forward when we get stuck, and by pressing through when we are hindered. Fighting builds up our strength. The simple secret of success in life is this: Take the hit, get back up, and press forward.

We feel average, as if there is no greatness available for us. The question becomes, who told you that? Who told you that you were average and not great? Who told you that you are ordinary and not worthy? You see, the journey to greatness begins on the inside. If you really believe you are mediocre, that means you are surrendering your best self; if you dare believe in your greatness, you believe that there is something more, that you deserve more. You wouldn't be reading this book if you didn't desire to reach for your inner awesomeness. For that inner strength that says there is something of significance within you. Take a step toward your **it** today, whatever that **it** may be. Once you start toward it, it will come toward you. The universe rewards those who reach for more.

By not leading a life on purpose we leave more on the table; life must be intentional and mapped out daily. Each 24 hours shapes our tomorrow. But it begins with our awareness, the awareness of each moment, each second, and each minute. You must wake up and say *this is what I want*! An awareness of what you want creates the possibility of achieving it. You must become one with yourself in order to win.

That means designing your day, creating your week, forming your month and crafting your new year. When that design is written on paper and is focused upon daily, it gives you emphasis to achieve it. Therefore, plan each day. This gives you the will to do it and makes up your mind to be able to do it.

As I look back on my years, with all its tears and fears, I often ask myself what I would tell the younger me. The me of 25 years ago, that is starting on this journey called life. As I look back at myself, I would want to realize the five things that I'm sharing with you now as well.

1. It's already in you, your power, your gift. The momentum to receive your dream, everything that you need to achieve it is already in you. That is the most important thing that you must learn.

2. Make **failure your friend**. It's okay to fail. Use it to your advantage and learn from each mistake.

3. Grow Yourself. When you grow, everything around you will grow. Your business will grow, your dream will grow, and all your plans will grow and become real. You're not in competition with anyone else; the competition is with life. When you grow, life grows with and for you.

4. Get connected to people ahead of you that are doing the things that you want to do, achieving the dreams that you want to achieve. Connect with them either consciously or even through their books and other material. Find a coach or mentor. Get in a growth environment.

5. Add Value to others. To add value to your life, you must add value to the lives of those around you. Value will always be significant in success.

With these five areas, you can achieve the dream that you want, and it will allow you to design the life that you desire and deserve!

Make the decision to live it. Make failure your friend. Continue to grow and work on yourself. Get connected with people who can push you toward your dream, and always add value to others.

My life has not been easy, but it is worth living. I am grateful that I have the opportunity to live my dreams and serve others by helping them live their dreams. Your dream is calling you and world is waiting for you to answer the call.

Bio:

Kim Ladson is one of the most dynamic personal development trainers of our time. She is a dynamic personality and a highly sought after motivator and speaker. She serves as one of John Maxwell's Certified Leadership Trainer and Coach as well as one of Les Brown's Platinum Speakers. She has a proven record of helping others achieve their best. She is charismatic, humorous and transformational. She teaches people how to go beyond their limitations and step into their unlimited possibilities. She has helped people from all walks of life harness their potential and reach a level of great success. She has also assisted organizations in achieving high performance by providing winning formulas and practical transformational strategies.

Contact info:

kimladson@aol.com

Postscript

Life is the essence of living. Freedom is living that life in excellence. This book has been the collaboration of success and the press involved with living that life. Ask yourself what is standing in your way from winning in life now. Ask yourself why you are still living beneath the privilege of your royal birth. The purpose of this book is to help you understand that you were designed to live life by design, not by default.

Drs. Kim and Anthony Ladson